The
Hoover Dam

A Monument of Ingenuity

The
Hoover Dam

A Monument of Ingenuity

★ ★ ★ Luke S. Gabriel

THE CHILD'S WORLD®, INC.

Library of Congress Cataloging-in-Publication Data
Gabriel, Luke S.
The Hoover Dam : a monument of ingenuity / by Luke S. Gabriel.
p.   cm.
Includes index.
Summary: Describes the history of the Hoover Dam,
why and how it was built, and how it works.
ISBN 1-56766-761-9
1. Hoover Dam (Ariz. and Nev.)—History—Juvenile literature.
[1. Hoover Dam (Ariz. and Nev.) 2. Dams.]   I. Title.
TC557.5.H6 G33   2000
627'.82'0979313—dc21   99-054206

Credits

© Ben D. Glaha/Bureau of Reclamation: 16, 19, 20, 23, 24
© Bettmann/CORBIS: 13
© Don Lowe/Tony Stone Images: 10
© 1993 Howard Garrett/Dembinsky Photo Assoc. Inc.: 6
© Jeff Greenberg/Visuals Unlimited: cover
© Mark E. Gibson/The Image Finders: 15
© Mark E. Gibson/Visuals Unlimited : 29
© Mark Newman/Visuals Unlimited: 26
© 1999 Michael E. Lubiarz/Dembinsky Photo Assoc. Inc.: 2
© Robert Cameron/Tony Stone Images: 30
© W.A. Davis/Bureau of Reclamation: 9

On the cover...

Front cover: From close up, Hoover Dam is an amazing sight.
Page 2: This is what Hoover Dam looks like from high above.

Table of Contents

"Look out! Flood!" These were the cries of the farmers in the Imperial Valley in California. The year was 1905. Huge rainstorms had caused the Colorado River to overflow. It flooded miles of farms, railroads, and buildings. A man named Blaine Hamann said, "The river was an enemy, and only in short periods of time could you look at it as a useful river. Most of the time it was something that would kill you or ruin your farm." In 1916 the river flooded California's Yuma Valley, ruining crops. Many people moved away forever. For people still living near the river, life was hard.

The Colorado River is a long river that twists and turns through the western United States. Many years ago, the Colorado River carved the *Grand Canyon.* In the early 1900s, because it caused so much flooding, people began to study ways to control the mighty river.

⇐ Here you can see boats as they travel down the Colorado River.

In 1918, an engineer named Arthur P. Davis recommended building a **dam** to control the river near Boulder Canyon. At Boulder Canyon, the river separates the states of Arizona and Nevada. In 1922, Davis gave his final report to the United States Congress. The report said the government could build the dam and then sell the electric power it produced to pay for the dam. In 1928, Congress approved the plan and President Calvin Coolidge signed it. Building the dam was about to begin!

**This is what Boulder Canyon looked ⇒
like before the dam was built.**

A dam stops water from flowing. Dams have been used to stop floods, make lakes, provide water for farms, and produce electricity. Dams are made of rock, dirt, or concrete. Concrete dams are the strongest. The dam on the Colorado River was to be made of concrete.

⇐ **Here you can see part of the huge concrete front of the dam.**

"Boom! Boom!" In 1931 the sound of explosions could be from heard miles away. Workers were putting dynamite into the walls of Boulder Canyon on both sides of the Colorado River. They were digging four huge tunnels to **divert** the river so the dam could be built.

Building the tunnels was not easy. At first, there were no roads into the Boulder Canyon area. Equipment, supplies, and workers had to be carried in by boat. Workers crossed the river on dangerous small bridges called **catwalks.** The catwalks were held up by steel cables. Cold winds blew through the canyon during the winter, dropping the temperature to near freezing. During the summer, the hot sun raised the temperature to over 120 degrees. But through it all, the tunnels had to be built.

These two men are walking across a high ⇒
catwalk over the construction site.

It took about 10 months to dig out the tunnels. The workers used 2,000 pounds of dynamite for every 14 feet. The tunnels were 56 feet wide and had a combined length of more than three miles. But were the tunnels ready?

No! The tunnels were not strong enough, and they were not watertight. It took another eight months to line the tunnels with concrete. Train tracks were laid down in the tunnels, and giant cranes rode on these tracks. The cranes helped workers frame the tunnels with steel and line the walls with concrete. When finished, the tunnels were lined with concrete three feet thick.

At the end of 1932, the tunnels were ready. Workers blocked the river by dumping tons of rocks into it. The water rose up and flowed into the tunnels. The river flowed through the tunnels and created a big dry spot in the bottom of Boulder Canyon. Now the dam could be built!

This picture was taken looking ⇒ down one of the huge tunnels.

"Look out below!" That was what a **high-scaler** would yell if rocks were falling. High-scalers were workers who used ropes to climb down the walls and cliffs of Boulder Canyon. Their job was to use dynamite, jackhammers, and other tools to clear away loose rock. They would also carry tools and other workers to places in the canyon that couldn't be reached any other way.

⇐ **This high-scaler is going over the side of the canyon to work on the dam.**

Being a high-scaler was dangerous. Many high-scalers were hurt or killed by falling rocks and tools. Some even fell into the canyon. To make their job safer, they invented their own hardhats. They used these hardhats until real hardhats could be brought in for them to use.

One time a man fell from the top of the canyon. A high-scaler swung out and caught him by the leg. Another high-scaler helped hold him until he could be lifted to safety. The high-scalers saved his life!

These high-scalers are drilling ⇒ into the canyon wall.

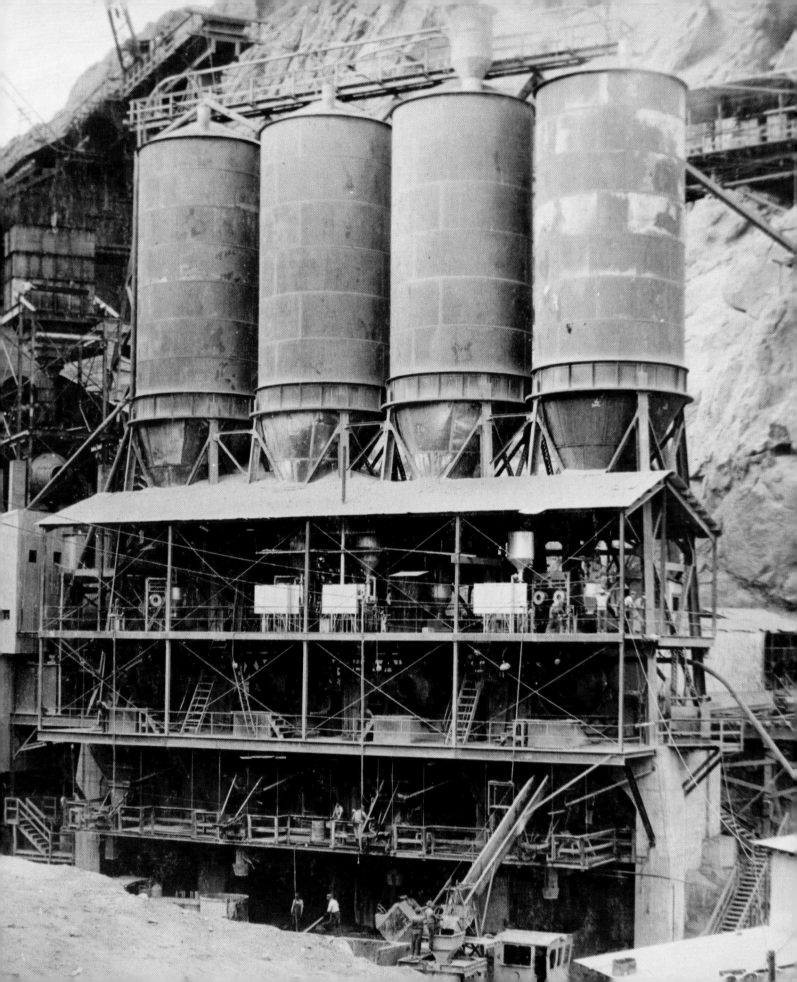

Where did the workers get all the concrete for lining the tunnels and building the dam? They made it themselves. Concrete is made of sand, water, cement, and crushed rock. Sand and water were easy to find, and cement could be brought in on trucks. But what about the crushed rock?

It took several months, but workers found a giant layer of rocks in Arizona six miles away from the dam site. Workers scooped the rocks onto trains and hauled them to the work site. The rocks were separated by size. Any rock over nine inches had to be crushed. The proper-sized rocks were then loaded onto other trains and hauled to the concrete mixing plant.

⇐ **This is one of the concrete mixing plants. If you look closely, you can see people working inside.**

As the months went by, more and more workers were needed to build the dam. The new workers had no place to live, so houses and a big dining hall were built. The dining hall could serve 6,000 meals every day. Every week the dining hall used about 60,000 eggs, 10,000 pounds of meat, and 24,000 pounds of fruits and vegetables. The workers and their families were hungry!

This growing town was named Boulder City. Although it wasn't fancy, Boulder City provided a nearby place for workers to live. It had no trees and it was very hot and dry. As more and more people moved in, schoolhouses, a hospital, a library, and a church were built.

This is what Boulder City looked like in 1933. ⇒

"Steady, steady!" The first concrete for the dam was poured on June 6, 1933. Workers poured concrete for almost two years. The last concrete was poured on May 29, 1935.

Pouring concrete wasn't an easy job. Cranes lifted the concrete in giant dump buckets. Workers had to move fast, or the concrete would harden in the dump bucket. Once a bucket was lifted to the right spot, the bottom opened and the concrete poured out. A crew of workers in rubber boots used shovels to smooth out the concrete. These workers were called **puddlers.** Being a puddler was probably the dirtiest job in the whole project!

⇐ **Here you can see puddlers hurrying to smooth the concrete pouring from the huge bucket.**   **25**

The concrete then had to set and harden. To help it set faster, the concrete was poured in small sections. It would take about three days for a five-foot section to harden. Then the next section could be poured on top of it. A mixture of cement and water called **grout** was then squeezed in between the sections. Grout was also squeezed into any cracks that were found. This made the entire dam watertight.

When finished, the dam was 726 feet tall. At the top it was 1,244 feet long and 45 feet wide. The dam was curved to make it stronger. The dam weighed more than 13 billion pounds. It was the heaviest concrete structure ever made!

⇐ **This picture was taken looking down over the top of the dam.**

Seventeen big machines called **turbines** were installed in the power plant section of the dam. Water flowing through the dam turned the turbines, producing electricity. This way of making electricity is called **hydroelectric power.** When the dam was built, it was the world's largest hydroelectric plant. The electricity was sold to electric companies that provided power to 1.3 million people in Nevada, Arizona, and California. The money from the electricity was more than enough to cover the entire cost of building the dam!

The water behind the dam is called a **reservoir.** This reservoir is named Lake Mead. Lake Mead is more than 550 feet deep in some places. It is 115 miles long and contains 9 trillion gallons of water! Each year, more than 9 million people visit Lake Mead to swim, boat, and fish.

These are the huge turbines ⇒
in the dam's power plant.

In September of 1935, President Franklin Roosevelt visited the opening of the dam. The dam was called Boulder Dam for many years. Some people suggested that the dam should be named after President Herbert Hoover. They suggested this because most of the work on the dam was completed while Hoover was president. In April of 1947, President Harry Truman renamed the dam Hoover Dam. That's the name it still has today.

Thousands of people visit Hoover Dam every year. There you can take a tour of the inside and walk across the top of the dam. Visitors can see the turbines and the tunnels, too. If you're near the Colorado River or Las Vegas, Nevada, don't forget to visit Hoover Dam!

Glossary

catwalks (KAT–woks)
Catwalks are small bridges hung in the air. Catwalks were used by the workers building Hoover Dam.

dam (DAM)
A dam is used to block the flow of water on a river. Hoover Dam was built to block the flow of the Colorado River.

divert (dy–VERT)
To divert a river means to change where the water flows. To build Hoover Dam, the Colorado River had to be diverted by tunnels.

grout (GROWT)
Grout is a cement and water mixture used to plug up cracks. Grout was used to plug up the cracks of Hoover Dam.

high-scaler (HY–skay-ler)
High-scalers were workers who hung from ropes to clear away loose rock from canyon walls. Many high-scalers helped to build Hoover Dam.

hydroelectric power (hy–droh–ee–LEK–trik POW–er)
Hydroelectric power is electricity produced by water flowing through a dam. Hoover Dam is a large producer of hydroelectric power.

puddlers (PUD–lerz)
A puddler was a type of concrete worker who smoothed wet concrete. Many puddlers helped pour the concrete of Hoover Dam.

reservoir (REH–zeh–vwar)
A reservoir is a lake created by damming up a river. Hoover Dam created the largest reservoir in the United States. It is called Lake Mead.

turbines (TUR–bynz)
Turbines are engines inside a dam that make hydroelectric power. Hoover Dam has 17 main turbines.

Index

Web Sites

Learn more about the Hoover Dam:

http://www.hooverdam.com

http://www.lc.usbr.gov/~pao/hoover.html

http://www.pbs.org/wgbh/pages/amex/hoover/